20th-Century Queer American History Reader

Tiny Topic Readers Humanities

Edited by
Bee Lehman and Emily Cole

Volume 2

20th-Century Queer American History Reader

Edited by
Samuel Hurwitz

DE GRUYTER
OLDENBOURG

This series' designers are committed to providing small readers with public domain material for survey courses in the Humanities disciplines, such as English and History. The goal is to have experts provide small selections of materials at low – or no – cost, which instructors can use for their course curriculum.

If you're interested in participating in the project, reach out to the series editors.

This series was designed in connection with Boston College's Collaborative Digital Projects Lab with funding from the Institute for Liberal Arts.

Series Editor: Bee Lehman, Ph.D. and Dr. Emily Cole, Ph.D.
Graphic Design: Franzi Paetzold and Dr. Emily Cole, Ph.D.

ISBN 978-3-11-155748-9
e-ISBN (PDF) 978-3-11-156092-2
e-ISBN (EPUB) 978-3-11-156100-4
ISSN 2944-1552

Library of Congress Control Number: 2025937521

Bibliographic information published by the Deutsche Nationalbibliothek
The Deutsche Nationalbibliothek lists this publication in the Deutsche Nationalbibliografie; detailed bibliographic data are available on the internet at http://dnb.dnb.de.

Cover image: Rodger Lehman, Untitled, 2024, painting, oil on canvas, private collection.
Typesetting: Integra Software Services Pvt. Ltd.
Printing and binding: CPI books GmbH, Leck

www.degruyterbrill.com
Questions about General Product Safety Regulation:
productsafety@degruyterbrill.com

Contents

List of Sources

https://doi.org/10.1515/9783111560922-203

Sources

Source 1: *Elaine Noble*, photograph, in *Public Officers of the Commonwealth of Massachusetts* (Boston, MA: General Court. 1976), 255. | Public Domain.

Introduction to LGBTQA+ US American History

The history of LGBTQ+ America begins before the arrival of European colonists. Many indigenous cultures of North America had relatively open social roles for queer men and women. Additionally, some indigenous societies were tolerant of berdaches who were individuals born male, but who dressed, lived and identified as women. These lax sexual and gender roles shocked many religiously conservative European colonists. After landing in Jamestown, Virginia in 1607 and later Plymouth, Massachusetts in 1620, colonists passed anti-sodomy and cross-dressing laws most likely because they were aware of queer and gender non-conforming behavior among their population and their indigenous neighbors. Additionally, through the scholarship of Richard Godbeer, there is ample evidence to suggest that many men during the early days of the American republic expressed strong intimate feelings of love and desire towards other men through public and private writings. These writings were not explicitly sexual in nature, but the ability for men to express deep love for other men in the late 18th and early 19th centuries would suggest that early America was to some extent tolerant of relationships that challenged the sexual and gender norms of religiously conservative America.

By the 19th century, many Americans began to become more familiar with instances of queer and gender non-conforming folks who asserted their presence in extraordinary ways. Jen Manion's book, *Female Husbands: A Trans History* recounted how newspapers regularly publicized the lives of certain Americans assigned female at birth who took up male names, dressed in male clothing and lived as men, even marrying women and taking up the role of husband. Manion revealed the relative frequency of this type of gender non-conformity happening all across the United States. Until they were outed by their community, these transgender men gained access to traditionally male jobs, partook in the conquest of the American West and lived their lives in relative obscurity in sparsely populated regions.

Queer and gender non-conforming life certainly did not remain behind closed doors in the first half of the 20th century. The appearance of LGBTQ+ individuals, especially queer men, in the historical record continued to grow, especially in urban centers. Peter Boag's *Same-Sex Affairs: Constructing and Controlling Homosexuality in the Pacific Northwest* highlighted how in cities like Portland, Oregon there were vibrant working-class and middle-class male homosexual subcultures. Urban neighborhoods and work camps attracted thousands of young and middle-aged men of various ethnic backgrounds who formed sexual and romantic relationships amongst themselves. On the other side of the country, in New York City,

https://doi.org/10.1515/9783111560922-001

George Chauncey's *Gay New York: Gender, Urban Culture, and the Making of the Gay Male World,* 1890–1940 uncovered lively multiracial lower to middle class homosexual subcultures that existed in neighborhoods such as Harlem and Greenwich Village.

Feminine-presenting men openly paraded down the streets of Manhattan in search of their next sexual encounter. In Harlem, the Hamilton Lodge Ball, a well-known annual masquerade ball popular with black and white community members, attracted drag queens, gay men, lesbians, transgender folks, and local celebrities. With industrialization, cities grew and so did the opportunities for queer and gender non-conforming men and women to meet and create spaces where they could socialize freely.

The latter half of the 20th century saw the formation of LGBTQ+ political consciousness. The Mattachine Society was founded in 1950 and advocated for the rights of gay men. Its lesbian counterpart, the Daughters of Bilitis, formed in 1955. The transgender rights movement began in 1960 with the publication of *Transvestia* magazine. Though, many consider the June 1969 Stonewall uprising as the moment where a sustained national gay rights movement in the U.S. began. Partly in response, annual LGBTQ+ rights protests swept through the country demanding civil and political rights. Many states began to decriminalize sodomy and to outlaw discrimination on the basis of sexual orientation. These civil rights victories were widely celebrated, though ultimately overshadowed by a deadly epidemic. The 1980s and 1990s witnessed the AIDS crisis, which became a new threat to LGBTQ+ movement, but especially to the gay and transgender communities, killing over 320,000 gay men and transgender men and women by the end of the century.

Source 2: John K. Hillers, *We-Wa, a Zuni Berdache, Weaving*, 1871-1907, photograph, NAID: 523796, National Archives at College Park. | Public Domain.

Many Indigenous groups in North America have their own understanding of gender, such as the third-gender category "two spirits" (Europeans used the offensive term *berdache*). Yet it is from European migrants, who often reacted to what they observed with prejudice, that we have most of the still-existing records on this and other gendered concepts.

Source 3:
Whitman did not publicly identify as homosexual; however, sexual attraction and affection toward men are central themes in his poetry.

Source 4:
Ella Wesner, a male impersonator (now often referred to as a drag king), performed during the latter 19th century on the vaudeville circuit. Wesner's personal life suggests that they might have identified as queer in the 21st century as opposed to "only" acting.

Source 5:
The Ladder was a monthly publication that ran from 1956 to 1972. It was the first lesbian publication circulated nationally in the U.S.

Source 3: Moses P. Rice, *Walt Whitman & His Rebel Soldier Friend Pete Doyle*, 1865, photograph, LC-USZ62-77004, Library of Congress. | No known restrictions on publication.

Source 4: Napoleon Sarony, *Ella Wesner*, 1873, postcard, JD Doyle Archives. | Public Domain.

The Ladder

OCTOBER, 1957

Source 5: *The Ladder*, October 1957, magazine cover, Internet Archive. | Public Domain.

Boston Queer History

The LGBTQ+ history of Boston mirrors much of the LGBTQ+ history of the rest of the United States. Queer and gender non-conforming individuals had to live their authentic selves mostly behind closed doors. Boston's image as a progressive, tolerant, queer-friendly city is a relatively new phenomenon. Nonetheless, there have been instances where Bostonians have broken with "traditional," heteronormative practices. For example, during much of the 18th century, intimate, same-sex relationships (especially among women) were sometimes encouraged and viewed as relatively innocuous. Because of the concept of separate spheres where men had "public" lives and women had "private" lives, close female bonding was tolerated and so, Boston marriages materialized. These were socially sanctioned relationships between well-off, independent women who lived together and supported one another. Contemporaries regarded these "marriages" as inoffensive and asexual, but historians of sexuality believe that many Boston marriages were cover for intimate same-sex relationships. Writers such as Emily Dickinson and Ralph Waldo Emerson praised these affectionate same-sex relationships. Though, by the turn of the 20th century, sexologists and researchers started to view Boston marriages and other similar cohabitations as a deviation from traditional gender and sexual norms and potentially dangerous to the well-being of society.

In Boston, anti-vice squads raided private gatherings of queer men and women, arresting them and charging them with lewd and indecent behavior. Police also frequently arrested transgender women, who were often soliciting sex in Back Bay and the South End, and charged them with being vagrants or being idle and disorderly. By the mid- to late-20th century, queer Bostonians had begun to build a politically conscious community. In 1969, a Boston chapter of the Mattachine Society was founded, which sponsored newsletters and lectures on the illegal treatment towards homosexuals. Four years later, Gay Community News began its weekly publication acting as a LGBTQ+ community newspaper and a platform for the gay liberation struggle. By the turn of the 21st century, Boston and Massachusetts had slowly become a more welcoming place for LGBTQ+ people. In 2003, the Massachusetts Supreme Judicial Court legalized same-sex marriage. Then, in 2011, Governor Deval Patrick signed House Bill 3810 which protected transgender people against discrimination. Boston has had a long anti-LGBTQ+ history, but through community activism, the city and state have begun to address the concerns of its LGBTQ+ residents.

https://doi.org/10.1515/9783111560922-002

Source 6: "*Good Evening Julian*," 1910, poster, JD Doyle Archives, Digital Transgender Archives. | Public Domain.

Source 6:
Julian Eltinge started a stage career as a child actor in Boston and went on to become famous for female impersonations. Eltinge appeared on stage and screen through the 1920s. Despite presenting a "delicate" femininity on stage and screen, Eltinge maintained an off-stage masculine persona. Contemporary reporters called Eltinge "ambisextrous."

Source 7:
Mrs. Annie Adams Fields and Miss Sarah Jewett lived together in a committed "Boston Marriage" for years at 148 Charles Street. Both were influential sources in Boston's literary scene as hostesses and writers.

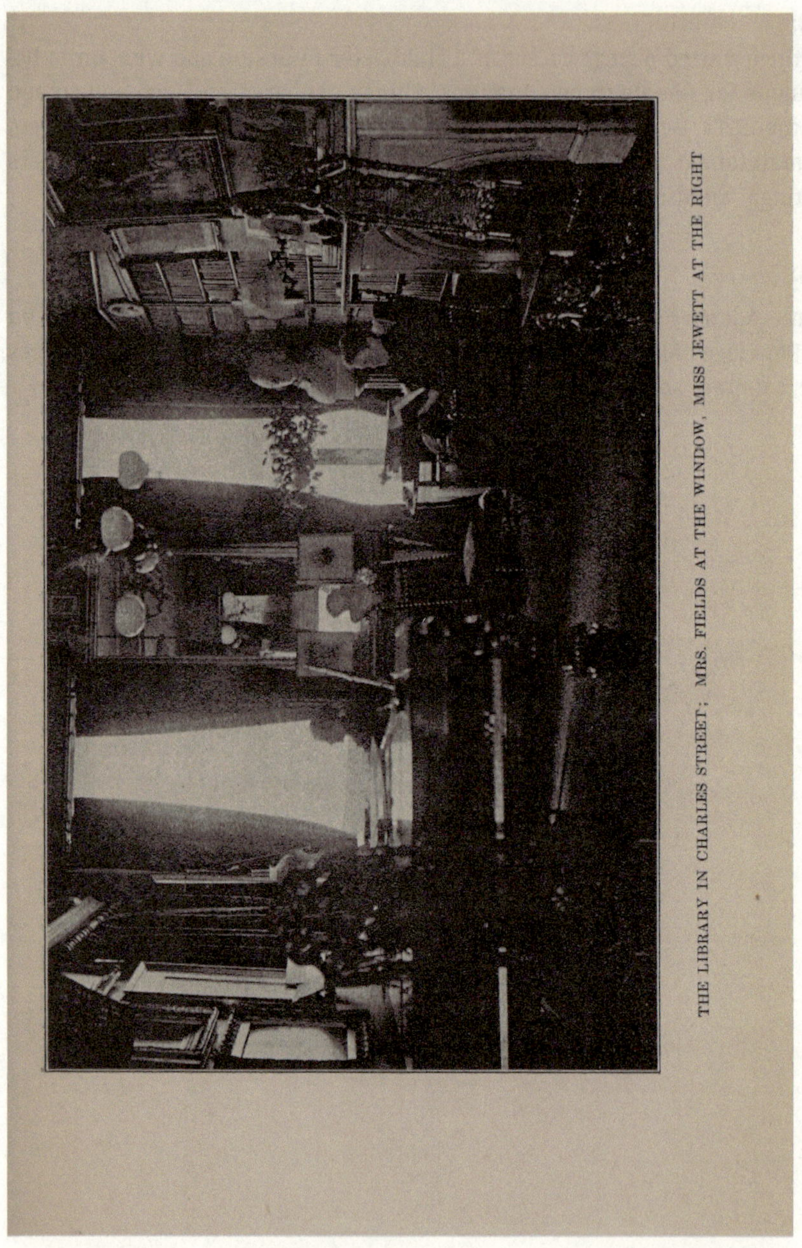

Source 7: *The Library in Charles Street; Mrs. Fields at the Window, Miss Jewett at the Right*, photograph, in M.A. De Wolfe Howe, *Memories of a Hostess* (Boston: Atlantic Month Press, 1922), HathiTrust. | Public Domain.

Do you remember, darling
  A year ago today
When we gave ourselves to each other
  Before you went away
At the end of that pleasant summer weather
Which we had spent by the sea together?

How little we knew, my darling,
  All that the year would bring!
Did I think of the wretched mornings
  When I should kiss my ring
And long with all my heart to see
The girl who gave the ring to me?

We have not been sorry darling
  We loved each other so-
We will not take back the promises
  We made a year ago-

And so again, my darling
  I give myself to you,
With graver thought than a year ago
  With love that is deep and true.

- Sarah Orne Jewett

Source 8: Sarah Orne Jewett, "Unpublished Love Poem," MS Am 1743.2–1743.27, Houghton Library, Harvard University. | Public Domain.

THE WANT OF YOU

A hint of gold where the moon wlll be ;
Through the flocking clouds just a star
or two ;
Leaf sounds soft and wet and hushed
And oh! the crying want of you.

EL BESO

Twlight—and you,
Quiet—the stars ;
Snare of the shine of your teeth.
Your provocatlve laughter,
The gloom of your hair ;
Lure of you eye and lip ;
Yearning, yearning,
Languor, surrender;
  Your mouth,
And madness, madness,
Tremulous, breathless, flaming,
The space of a sigh ;
Then awakening—remembrance,
Pain, regret—your sobbing ;
And again quiet—the stars,
Twilight—and you.

- Angelina W. Grimké

Source 9: Angelina W. Grimké, "The Want of You," in *Negro Poets and Their Poems*, ed. by Robert Thomas Kerlin (Washington, D.C.: Associated Publishers, 1923), 152, 154. | Public Domain.

Source 10: Betsy Graves Reyneau, *Alain Locke*, ca. 1943–1963, painting, NARA – 559203, National Archives at College Park. | Public Domain.

Source 11: Kevin Lynch, Gyorgy Kepes, and Nishan Bichajian, *Subway Entrance at Park Street, 8.00 P.M.*, 1954–1959, photograph, MIT Libraries. |

Source 12: Kevin Lynch, Gyorgy Kepes, and Nishan Bichajian, *Corner of Avery Street and Washington Street*, 1954–1959, photograph, MIT Library. | Creative Commons Attribution-NonCommercial 3.0.

Source 10:
Alain Locke, "Dean" of the Harlem Renaissance, attended Harvard before teaching at Howard. Locke openly identified as homosexual.

Source 11:
In the 1920s, queer spaces began to appear around Boston in the form of speakeasies like Crawford House. Between the 1930s and 1940s, the number of safe spaces expanded with institutions like The Punch Bowl.

Source 12:
By the 1950s – despite the Lavendar Scare – queer life in Boston had a vibrant presence with places like the Waldorf Restaurant, Jacques, and the Napolean Club.

Source 13:
The map on page 18 is the east half of a 1962 city map of Boston. It includes an outline of the "Combat Zone" as well as highlighting the locations shown in the previous two Sources: Subway at Park Street and Avery at Washington. The locations of the next two Sources (Playground Café and the location of the 1971 protest march) are also marked.

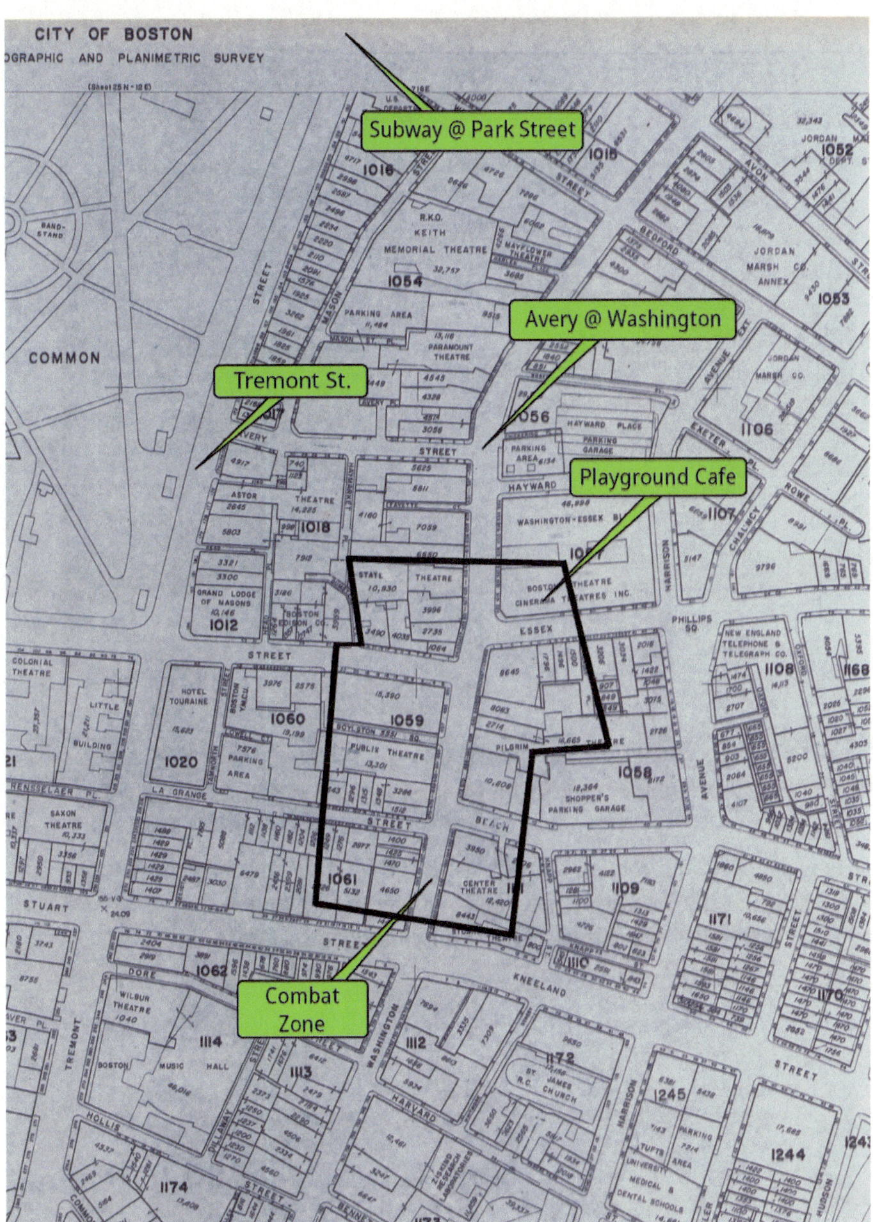

Source 13: East half of Lockwood, Kessler & Bartlett and Fairchild Aerial Surveys, inc., *City of Boston: Topographic and Planimetric Survey*, map, 1: 1,200 (Boston: Boston Redevelopment Authority, 1962), G1234.B6 C58 1962, Norman B. Leventhal Map Center Collection. | Public Domain, courtesy of Norman B. Leventhal Map & Education Center.

Source 14: City of Boston, *Playground Café*, 1960s, photograph, Mayor John Collins Collection, Boston City Archives. | Copyright City of Boston.

The Playground Cafe opened at 21 Essex Street in 1937 in a downtown area formerly known as the "Combat Zone," near Scollay Square (now Government Center). The bar served parts of the queer community until its closure in 1998.

Source 15: John Kyper, *Marchers near Tremont Street*, June 26, 1971, photograph, History Project. | Used with permission from photographer.

Recollections of Boston's Gay M

I moved to Boston in June, 1969. Vermont had seemed to be in the radical bush leagues, and I wanted to go where "the Movement" was. (The state has changed a lot since then, and I often toy with the thought of moving back. Maybe I will, yet.) But 1969 was the year of the fatal SDS split, and I found what was left of the movement furiously ripping itself to shreds, fighting over incredibly obscure differences of dogma. I thought I was watching medieval theologians debating thenumber of angels on a pin! (Some gay groups, alas, have been no less susceptible to such sectarian nonsense: Witness the split several years ago in the Lavender and Red Union, and its quarreling progeny in the Sparticist League and the Revolutonary Socialist League.) Reconstructing a militarist society was going to take more than the substitution of one male power trip for another.

I was drunk with this exposure to gay energy, and I went to Sporters nearly every night for a month. But I quickly tired of standing around for hours in a cramped, smoky room, staring at other men and trying in my shyness to start a conversation with a stranger without feeling like a fool. I soon tired of the game. In January, 1970, an ad in *Boston After Dark* for people interested in starting a Student Homophile League got me in touch with Stan Tillotson.

The Homophile Union of Boston (HUB), the city's first established gay organization, started in January, 1969, in Frank Morgan's Dorchester living room. (I always admired Frank for having the guts to come out in the community where he had grown up.) By the end of the year there were also the Boston University Homophile Club, which soon expanded to become the area-wide Student Homophile League (SHL) and a chapter of the Daughters of Bilitis (DOB). Appropriately, this Puritan-Catholic city that was notorious for banning books until a generation ago, had little history of homophile organization. Attempts to form a local Mattachine Society in the 1950s had floundered because of the abrasive personality of Prescott Townsend, its eccentric Yankee Brahmin founder.

Source 16: Snippets from "Recollections of Boston's Gay Movement," *Gay Community News* 7, no. 42 (May 17, 1980): 1, 13, History Project. | Used with permission from author.

ovement

The first action of Boston's GLF was to march as a contingent in the April Moratorium on Boston Common. At its height there were about 100 of us, including a number of feminist supporters. Our signs — "Bring the Boys Home/Gay Liberation Front" — scandalized many people, including some gays. I continued to hear about it for several years thereafter. Unfortunately, our contingent was only one bright spot amid a lot of gloom: Th
October counterpart six
and anger over Nixon's d
furious riot in which peo
not, even in my nonviol
shared and were expressi
was savagely attacked v
members of an antiwar g
keeping the protest Resp
San Francisco brought
earlier riot.

John Kyper

Source 16 (continued)

100 Franklin St., Boston
Massachusetts 02110
telephone 617 426-3325
John W. Roberts,
Executive Director

An affiliate of the
American Civil Liberties
Union

CIVIL LIBERTIES UNION OF MASSACHUSETTS

July 30, 1975

TO: President Gerald R. Ford
Secretary of Defense James Schlesinger
The Massachusetts Congressional Delegation

FROM: Ellen Feingold, President
Civil Liberties Union of Massachusetts

The Civil Liberties Union of Massachusetts opposes the Department of Defense's policy of separating from the service persons who engage in homosexual activity.

The right to privacy in relations between consenting adults is a fundamental liberty guaranteed by the Constitution and federal privacy legislation, which cannot be abridged by Department of Defense regulations.

The Armed Services must recognize that there is no correlation between a soldier's sexual preference and his ability to perform his duties capably. The Army's attempts to discharge PFC Barbara Randolph and PV2 Debbie Watson after both had served as members of an honor platoon at Fort Devens is the kind of discrimination that has been declared illegal when applied to religious or ethnic minorities.

At a time when the civilian sector is demonstrating an increased tolerance towards private sexual activity, the Armed Services should strive to eliminate discrimination, rather than perpetuate its prejudicial and unjust regulations.

The Civil Liberties Union urges you to impress upon the Armed Forces its responsibility, as a branch of the federal government, to educate its members to respect the privacy and individual differences of others and not to encourage bigotry, intolerance and arbitrary invasions of privacy.

Ellen Feingold

Ellen Feingold
President

Source 17: Ellen Feingold to Gerald R. Ford, Civil Liberties Union, July 30, 1975, Carton 63 Civil Liberties Union of Mass archival records II CLUM subject files, 192–1987, Massachusetts Historical Society. | Courtesy of the MHS.

Source 17:
Letter from ACLU protesting the military discharge of two gay female soldiers on account of their sexual preferences.

Source 19:
Founded in 1973, *Gay Community News* (GNC) was published weekly in Boston until 1992, then quarterly until 1999. GNC began as a small community newsletter with a calendar of events. It quickly expanded to national coverage of the gay liberation and lesbian and gay rights movements. A respected if controversial publication, GNC often became a catalyst for political debate.

Source 20:
The City of Boston would see several cases examining the right of free expression of Queer individuals and the right to express their identities in public. Irish-American Gay, Lesbian and Bisexual Group of Boston et al. v. City of Boston was just one of many cases.

Source 18: *Boston Bisexual Women's Network*, photograph, 3x5in, Boston Bisexual Women's Network, Lesbian Herstory Archives. | Courtesy of Lesbian Herstory Archives.

Winter 1995 | Volume 20, No. 4 | $3.50

GAY COMMUNITY NEWS

Reading between the lines

USED TO AGITATE WHITE PEOPLE AGAINST CIVIL RIGHTS

Source 19: *Gay Community News* 20. No. 04, Winter 1995, newspaper cover, History Project. | Courtesy of the History Project.

COMMONWEALTH OF MASSACHUSETTS

SUPREME JUDICIAL COURT

NO. SJC 06498

IRISH-AMERICAN GAY, LESBIAN and BISEXUAL
GROUP OF BOSTON, et al.

Plaintiffs-Appellants

v.

CITY OF BOSTON

Defendant-Appellee

v.

JOHN J. HURLEY, INDIVIDUALLY, and THE SOUTH BOSTON
ALLIED WAR VETERANS COUNCIL

Defendants-Appellants

In his letter, Dimino referenced the controversy that had arisen in March of 1992, immediately before the 1992 Parade, concerning whether the plaintiffs would be permitted by the Veterans to march and the fact that the court (Zobel, J.) had on March 11, 1992, only four days before the Parade, issued an order allowing the plaintiffs to march. *Irish American Gay, Lesbian and Bisexual Group of Boston v. City of Boston, et als.*, C.A. No. 92-1518 (Suffolk Super. Ct. March 11, 1992, Zobel, J.) (hereinafter "the 1992 Order"). Therefore, the BTD sought from the Veterans a statement as to whether they intended to conduct the 1993 Parade in a manner consistent with the 1992 order. Ex. 7, A. 601; FFRL, Add. B-13.

Source 20: Irish-American Gay, Lesbian and Bisexual Group of Boston et al. v. City of Boston et al. case files (Parade Case), #0700.022, City of Boston Archives. | Courtesy of the City of Boston Archives.

Source 21: Two photographs from Isabel Leon, *Pride Lights in the South End*, May 8, 2004, photograph, City of Boston Archives, https://archives.boston.gov. | In copyright – Non-commercial use permitted. Reproduction courtesy of Boston City Archives.

US American Queer History

Repression and secrecy reigned supreme in how many queer and gender non-conforming individuals behaved throughout the United States. However, the fight for LGBTQ+ rights did not remain behind closed doors. In 1924, Henry Gerber founded the Society for Human Rights which was the first gay rights organization in America. This organization sought to promote and protect the civil liberties of gay men. The Society for Human Rights, however, only lasted a year before being disbanded due to the arrests of its members. The Mattachine Society, founded in 1950, would be the first sustained national gay rights organization. But, gay men and women continued to live under duress.

In World War Two, tens of thousands of queer veterans obtained a blue discharge because of their sexuality. This discharge cut off thousands of gay veterans from the benefits of the 1944 G.I. Bill. The 1950s would be a decade of intense persecution of gay men and women. A senate report issued in 1950 designated gay federal government employees as security risks. Two years later, the American Psychiatric Association labeled homosexuality as a personality disorder. The general public considered queerness not only an illness, but a direct threat to American democracy. This oppressive environment continued well into the next decade. It was not until the 1969 Stonewall Riots that America's modern LGBTQ+ rights movement began. The 1970s saw some positive incremental changes to gay rights. The American Psychiatric Association removed homosexuality as a mental illness. Openly gay politicians began to win local and state elections and tens of thousands of queer and gender non-conforming Americans participated in the National March on Washington for Lesbian and Gay Rights. These victories, however, were quickly overshadowed by the 1980s and 1990s. The AIDS crisis ravaged the gay and transgender communities and killed hundreds of thousands of LGBTQ+ Americans. By the end of the 20th century, the AIDS crisis began to subside due to new medication and prevention awareness.

The 21st century has seen an increase of acceptance of queer and gender non-conforming people. For example, by 2015 a majority of Americans supported same-sex marriage, which was reflected in the law when the U.S. Supreme Court legalized same-sex marriage. By the early 21st century, openly gay Americans were serving as governors, U.S. senators, representatives, and members of the president's cabinet.

https://doi.org/10.1515/9783111560922-003

Source 22: Alice Austen, *Trude and I, Masked, Short Skirts*, August 6, 1891, photograph, Staten Island Historical Society. | Public Domain.

Alice Austen (186–1952) lived during a period in which it was largely unacceptable to openly identify as queer in any capacity. Nonetheless, based on Austen's art, scholars largely believe that Austen was either a lesbian or woman-loving. Yet, because there is no record of Austen actively identifying as such, placing her in these categories becomes questionable.

Source 23: Charles Demuth, *Turkish Bath with Self Portrait*, 1918, painting. | Public Domain.

Source 24: J.C. Leyendecker, *Arrow Collars & Shirts*, 1913, advertisement, USPO-P, registration no. 3428, Library of Congress. | No known restrictions on publication.

Source 24 (continued)

Episode

I have robbed the garrulous streets,
Thieved a fair girl from their blight,
I have stolen her for a sacrifice
That I shall make to this mysteried night.
I have brought her, laughing,
To my quietly sinister garden.
For what will be done there
I ask no man's pardon.

I brush the rouge from her cheeks,
Clean the black kohl from the rims
Of her eyes; loose her hair;
Uncover the glimmering, shy limbs.
I break wild roses, scatter them over her.
The thorns between us sting like love's pain.
Her flesh, bitter and salt to my tongue,
I taste with endless kisses and taste again.
At dawn I leave her
Asleep in my wakening garden.

(For what was done there
I ask no man's pardon.)

- Elsa Gidlow

Source 25: Elsa Gidlow, "Episode," in *On a Grey Thread* (Chicago: Will Ransom, 1923). | Public Domain.

Source 25:

Gidlow also published an autobiography in the late 1980s: *Elsa, I Come with My Songs: The Autobiography of Elsa Gidlow* with Booklegger Press, 1986. It was one of the first queer autobiographies published without a pseudonym.

Source 26:

Hart Crane is thought to have written the multi-part “Voyages” as a reflection of a passionate relationship with a sailor in New York City.

Source 27:

Original record is a printed photograph of a bulletin board with multiple pieces of ephemera. This photograph of the Ball is one of those pieces of ephemera.

Voyages
I

Above the fresh ruffles of the surf
Bright striped urchins flay each other with sand.
They have contrived a conquest for shell shucks,
And their fingers crumble fragments of baked
weed
Gaily digging and scattering.

And in answer to their treble interjections
The sun beats lightning on the waves,
The waves fold thunder on the sand;
And could they hear me I would tell them:

O brilliant kids, frisk with your dog,
Fondle your shells and sticks, bleached
By time and the elements; but there is a line
You must not cross nor ever trust beyond it
Spry cordage of your bodies to caresses
Too lichen-faithful from too wide a breast.
The bottom of the sea is cruel.

- Hart Crane

Source 26: Hart Crane, "Voyages: I," in *White Buildings: Poems* (New York: Boni & Liveright, 1926), 49. | Public Domain.

Source 27: Portion of photograph of bulletin board, Jessie Tarbox Beals, *Webster Hall Ball*, 1920s, photograph, Schlesinger Library. | Jessie Tarbox Beals, courtesy of Schlesinger Library.

B.D. Woman Blues (1935)

Comin' a time, B.D.women they ain't going to need no men,
Comin' a time, B.D. women they ain't going to need no men,
'Cause the way they treat us is a lowdown and dirty sin.

B.D. women, you sure can't understand,
B.D. women, you sure can't understand,
They got a head like a sweet angel and they walk just like a natural man.

B.D. women, they all done learned their plan,
B.D. women, they all done learned their plan,
They can lay their jive just like a natural man.

B.D. women, B.D. women, you know they sure is rough,
B.D. women, B.D. women, you know they sure is rough,
They all drink up plenty whiskey and they sure will strut their stuff.

B.D. women, you know they work and make their dough,
B.D. women, you know they work and make their dough,
And when they get ready to spend it, they know they have to go.

- written and sung by Lucille Bogan

Source 28: Lucille Bogan, "B.D. Woman Blues," 1935, lyrics. | Public Domain.

Billy Strayhorn was among the most influential composers of the Harlem Renaissance with works like "A Train."

Source 29: William P. Gottlieb, [*Portrait of Billy Strayhorn, New York, N.Y., between 1946 and 1948*], 1946, photograph, 2023868295, Library of Congress. | Public Domain.

Source 30: *Buddy Kent*, [1940], flyer, Lesbian Herstory Archives. | Courtesy of Herstory Archive.

Source 30:
Buddy Kent would reign as one of the New York City drag kings between the 1940s and the 1960s.

Source 31:
Arthur Gold and Robert Fizdale met at Julliard and formed a lifelong intimate and working relationship. As one of the most prominent piano duos of the 20th century, the two worked with John Cage and notable musicians and composers. Later in life, Gold and Fizdale wrote food articles and hosted a cooking show. Their papers are held at the Julliard School.

Source 32:
Christine Jorgensen was an actress, singer, recording artist, transgender activist, and veteran. Jorgensen underwent sex reassignment surgery in Denmark in 1952. Upon return to the United States, her transition made front-page news. Jorgensen promoted transgender awareness.

Source 31: Carl Van Vechten, [*Portrait of Arthur Gold and Robert Fizdale*], January 4, 1952, photograph, Lot 12735, Van Vechten Collection, Library of Congress. | Public Domain.

CHRISTINE PLANS MARRIAGE

Christine Jorgensen, the boy turned girl, and Howard J. Knox, 33, of Waukegan, Ill., stand in New York's Municipal Building after failing to get a marriage license because Mr. Knox couldn't produce an Illinois divorce decree which ended a previous marriage. He said he'll arrange to obtain one.—AP Wirephoto.

Source 32: "Christine Plans Marriage," *Evening Star*, March 31, 1959, Chronicling America. | Public Domain.

Source 33: Warren K. Leffler, [*Bayard Rustin at News Briefing on the Civil Rights March on Washington in the Statler Hotel, Half-Length Portrait, Seated at Table*], August 27, 1963, photograph, LC-DIG-ppmsc -01272, Library of Congress. | No known restrictions on publication.

Source 34: *Lesbians Unite: Graffiti on 3rd Street*, 1968, photograph, Photo files, Arcus Flynn folder, Lesbian Herstory Archives. | Courtesy Lesbian Herstory Archive.

Source 35: *Sylvester Performing with Backup Singers, Circa 1970–1980*, photograph, Sylvester Collection, 201–05, GLBT Historical Society. | Courtesy of the GLBT Historical Society.

Source 36: *Transvestia* 1, no.5 (July 1960), magazine cover, Transgender Archives, University of Victoria. | Courtesy of Transgender Archives.

Source 36:
Transvestia was published from 1960 to 1986 “by, for and about transvestites to provide them with: Entertainment–Education–Expression by means of fiction, articles of opinion, true experiences etc. Its purpose is to help its readers to promote: Understanding–Acceptance–Peace of Mind. Its policy is to limit its scope of coverage and interest to the field of the heterosexual transvestite.” (Transvestia, no.25, 1964). Full text online.

Source 37:
On the one-year anniversary of the Stonewall Riots, June 28, 1970, Lilli Vincenz took a video camera to the first of the Christopher Street Day Liberation Parades. The parade wound along 50 blocks and was observed by thousands of supporters.

Source 38:
Vanguard, founded by LGBTQ+ youth of the Tenderloin district of San Francisco in the 1960s, covered topics such as queer politics, poverty among LGTBQ+ youth, and gender and sexuality.

Source 37: Screenshots of *Gay and Proud*, documentary, 1970, Library of Congress. | No known restrictions on publication.

Source 38: *Vanguard Magazine: The Magazine of the Tenderloin* 3, no. 2, 1970, magazine cover, GLBT Historical Society. | Courtesy GLBT Historical Society.

Source 39: *LHEF Contingent*, ca 1970, photograph, Photo Files, Marches 70s Folder, Lesbian Herstory Archives. | Courtesy Lesbian Herstory Archive.

Source 40: *I Never Loved a Man the Way That I Love You! Gay Pride Week*, 1973, poster, Yanker poster collection, Library of Congress. | No known restrictions on publication.

Source 41: Bettye Lane, *The Blacker the Berry the Sweeter the Dyke*, Black Lesbian Caucus, June 1973, photograph, Lesbian Herstory Archives. | Copyright Bettye Lane, courtesy Lesbian Herstory Archives.

Source 42: Warren K. Leffler, [*Gay Rights Demonstration*], July 11, 1976, photograph, LC-U9- 32917-36 [P&P], Library of Congress. | No known restrictions on publication.

Source 43: Radical Women (Seattle, Wash.), *A New Era for Women Workers, Minority Women and Lesbians*, 1976, poster, POS 6 – US, no. 992 (C size) [P&P], Library of Congress. | No known restrictions on publication.

Source 44: *Poetry Collection*, 1978, covers, 4x5in., Photo Files, Lesbian Herstory Archives. | Courtesy Lesbian Herstory Archives.

The Black Lesbian Newsletter, later renamed Onyx, first appeared in the early 1980s. The newsletter focused on themes and topics concerning black lesbians.

Source 45: Onyx, *Black Lesbian Newsletter*, August 1982, periodical cover, #GLBT-PER, GLBT Historical Society. | Courtesy of GLBT Historical Society.

Source 46: Maxine Wolfe, *End Lesbian Oppression*, 1982, photograph, Graffiti photo files, Lesbian Herstory Archives. | Photo by Maxine Wolfe, courtesy Lesbian Herstory Archives.

Source 47: *King of the Crystal Palace*, 1983, Promotional Flyer, C.D. Arnold Papers, #200–58, GLBT Historical Society. | Creative Commons: Attribution-NonCommercial-NoDerivs, Reprinted with permission from GLBT Historical Society.

Source 48: *barcard1*, September 1984, photograph, 4x5in., graphics, Lesbian Herstory Archives. | Photo by Saskia Scheffer courtesy Lesbian Herstory Archives.

Source 49: Saskia Scheffer, *Shrine*, November 1992, photograph, 4x5in., Photofiles, Lesbian Herstory Archives. | Photo by Saskia Scheffer courtesy of Lesbian Herstory Archives.

Source 50: Carol M. Highsmith, AIDS Quilt, Washington, D.C., 1980, Transparency, 2006, LC-HS503- 2457, Library of Congress. | No known restrictions on publication.

In 1987, a small group of people gathered to begin documenting those lost to the AIDS epidemic by representing their lost ones with quilted panels. It included 1,920 panels when it was displayed at the National Mall later that year and had grown to 48,000 panels by 2012. The quilt is available online at the National Aids Memorial (https://www.aidsmemorial.org/interactive-aids-quilt).

Grace and Lace Letter

A Christian Journal
For Crossdressers, Crossgendered,
and Transsexual Persons

Post Office Box 31253
Jackson, MS 39286-1253

Source 51: Lee Frances Heller, *Grace and Lace Letter: A Christian Journal for Crossdressers, Crossgendered, and Transsexual Persons*, 1990s, newsletter cover, Transgender Archives, University of Victoria. | Courtesy of Transgender Archives.

Source 52: *Finocchio's Flyer*, 1999, promotional material, Finocchio's Collection, 199–79, GLBT Historical Society. | Courtesy of GBLT Historical Society.

Gathering places for expression, meetings, and conversation are essential for community development. Based in San Francisco, Finocchio's has boasted providing space for "female impersonation and illusion [. . .] since 1936."

Source 53: *Transgender Tapestry*, Summer 2003, magazine cover, Transgender Archives, University of Victoria.| Courtesy of Transgender Archives.

Source 54: *Lesbian Herstory Archives Newsletter*, Fall 2001, newsletter cover, Lesbian Herstory Archives. | Courtesy of Lesbian Herstory Archives.

Source 55: *Bay Area American Indian Two Spirits, 1st Annual Two-Spirit Powwow Flyer*, February 2012, poster, GLBT Historical Society. | Courtesy of GLBT Historical Society.

Source 55:
The Bay Area American Indian Two Spirits group aims to "restore and recover" the two spirit identity.

Source 56:
Sign for the Gay '90s, a gay bar and dance club in downtown Minneapolis.

Source 56: Carol M. Highsmith, *Sign for the Gay '90s*, February 16, 2020, photograph, Library of Congress. | No known restrictions.

Source 57: Rodger Lehman, *Whippets*, 2020s, painting, personal collection. | Reproduced with permission from artist.

Source 57 (continued)

Collections Focused on Boston

The Arthur and Elizabeth Schlesinger Library at Harvard University

3 James St, Cambridge, MA 02138, https://www.radcliffe.harvard.edu/schlesinger-library

The Schlesinger Library has a multitude of LGBTQ+ related personal papers and materials, newsletters and magazines. Much of its materials are not digitized and are stored offsite. It is important to contact the library ahead of a visit in order to request access to many of their items, as a significant portion of their materials consist of the personal papers of 20th-century LGBTQ+ feminists, political and social activists, and academics. The library also contains newsletters and magazines that deal with gay, lesbian, bisexual, and transgender topics. Lastly, it should be noted that only some of its collections concern Boston's LGBTQ+ community. Most of its materials are nationally focused.

Collection descriptions excerpted from Schlesinger Library's "Research Guides: LGBTQ+: Magazines & Newsletters," accessed November 25, 2024, https://guides.library.harvard.edu/.

Aché: The Bay Area's Journal for Black Lesbians

https://hollis.harvard.edu/
"Longest-running African American lesbian journal and was published from 1989 to 1993."

The Advocate

https://hollis.harvard.edu/
"A United States national gay and lesbian newsmagazine [sic] averaging 130 pages per issue containing fiction and nonfiction articles, local and national news, and reviews of books and entertainment as well as photographs. This is one of the most-read national gay and lesbian publications with regular features including letters, editorials, articles on travel, entertainment, and gay culture around the world."

https://doi.org/10.1515/9783111560922-004

Anything that Moves

https://hollis.harvard.edu/ or available on the Internet Archive

Published from 1990 to 2002 in San Francisco, “The magazine’s mission was to confront and redefine concepts of sexuality and gender, to defy stereotypes and cookie-cutter definitions of bisexuals and to combat biphobia.”

***Atlanta* (Atlanta Lesbian Feminist Alliance)**

https://hollis.harvard.edu/

“A southeast U.S. lesbian and feminist newsletter averaging 16 pages per issue containing nonfiction articles, local, club, and national news, and reviews of interest to lesbians with black and white illustrations in 22 by 28 cm format. Regular features include “Ask Aunt Luna” and a calendar of events. ALFA is concerned with the entire spectrum of lesbian-feminist issues from discrimination to the rights and needs of fat and differently-abled women.”

Black/out*: *The Magazine of the National Coalition of Black Lesbians and Gays

https://hollis.harvard.edu/

“An international black gay and lesbian magazine averaging 40 pages per issue including fiction and nonfiction articles and national news with black and white illustrations in 14 by 22 cm format. Regular features include “Viewpoint”, national news, cover features, and directory. Each issue is centered around a theme. The publication is intended ‘to provide equal discussion of any issues that affect the lives, struggles, and achievements of the black and third world people of color community.’” The publication is out of Chicago, IL.

Dike

https://hollis.harvard.edu/

This magazine features articles on “theoretical politics, live events, place, current and past history, media, fashions, music, home economics, literature, animal lore, health, applied sciences and gossip. Covers Lesbian culture and straight culture; Straight culture is present in our lives and in our minds. It is violent and perverted. We recognize and analyze it and in this way prevent it from retarding our growth. We believe separatism demands constant vigilance and analysis.”

Ginger

https://hollis.harvard.edu/

Started in 2003 and published in Somerville, MA, *Ginger* is a "personal zine about Cory, a lesbian anarchist in her early twenties and who grew up poor, who writes about her pregnancy, including her artificial insemination, and gives DIY recommendations for other pregnant women."

Robin Bernstein Collection (b. 1969)

https://hollis.harvard.edu/

"Robin Bernstein was a professor of History, African American Studies, and Studies of Women, Gender, and Sexuality at Harvard University. Bernstein's research focuses on childhood, theater and performance, and race in the United States. This collection includes newsletters, documents, and programs from lesbian organizations and queer theater productions, including a 1991 "Statement of Principles" from Lesbians for Lesbians, a Greenfield, Massachusetts, organization. It also includes audiotapes and phonograph records, primarily featuring lesbian comedians."

Charlotte Bunch Collection (b. 1944)

https://hollis.harvard.edu/

"Active in the women's liberation movement of the 1960s, Bunch taught courses on feminism at colleges and universities, participated in international conferences concerning women, peace, and Christianity, edited feminist books and journals, and worked to develop a lesbian/feminist ideology."

Barbara Deming Collection (191–1984)

https://hollis.harvard.edu/

"Author and activist Barbara Deming began her career writing theater and film reviews, poetry, short stories, and a novel. In 1959, inspired by Gandhi's writings, Deming became politically active, advocating nonviolence in all spheres of life. Periodicals such as *The Nation and Liberation* (for which she was an editor) published many of her political essays. She demonstrated for peace and civil rights and was jailed several times for acts of civil disobedience. In the early 1970s, she became a feminist and worked on women's and lesbian issues until her death in 1984."

Barbara Hoffman Collection (ca. 193–2015)
https://hollis.harvard.edu/
"A clinical psychologist and activist for lesbian, gay, bisexual, and transgender rights, Barbara Rodamer Hoffman graduated from Radcliffe College (AB 1957), where she helped organize the Lesbian Alumnae of Radcliffe College, a precursor to the Harvard Gay and Lesbian Caucus. She received a master's and doctorate from Boston University and worked for the Massachusetts Department of Mental Health."

Massachusetts Historical Society

1154 Boylston St, Boston, MA 02215
Massachusetts Historical Society has a collection related to the history of sexuality. The collection covers topics such as "sexual desire and behavior, legal classifications and cases involving sex and sexuality (such as adultery, fornication, and sodomy), criminalization of sexuality. sexual and gender nonconformity, same-sex desires and relationships, gay rights, HIV/AIDS, sexual violence, sex work, sex education, pornography, religion and sexuality, birth control and abortion, and childbirth." These materials are not digitized and will need to be accessed in person.

Collection descriptions drawn from "Collection Guides," Massachusetts Historical Society, accessed 2024, https://www.masshist.org/collection-guides/.

American Civil Liberties Union of Massachusetts records, 192–2005
https://www.masshist.org/
Predominately focused on the 1970s through 1990s, "This collection includes materials on gay rights (1970s-1980s), sex education (1970s, 1990s), sex offenders, abortion (1970s-1980s), the right wing on sex, and midwifery (1980s), as well as materials relating to homosexuality and the military, particularly CLUM's involvement in a 1975 case at Fort Devens in Massachusetts and more."

Gerry E. Studds papers, 194–2008
https://www.masshist.org/
"This collection consists of the papers of the first openly gay member of the U.S. Congress, Gerry E. Studds (193–2006). The collection includes material relating to gay rights (including military service) and HIV/AIDS."

The History Project

565 Boylston St, Boston, MA 02116
"The History Project is focused exclusively on documenting and preserving the history of New England's LGBTQ communities and sharing that history with LGBTQ individuals, organizations, allies, and the public." It contains digitized and non-digitized collections. Some of its collections consist of AIDS ephemera, the Homophile Union of Boston papers, and the Student Homophile League of Boston

collection. This archive also houses hundreds of hours of oral interviews of LGBTQ+ Bostonians.

Collection descriptions drawn from "Collections," History Project, accessed 2024, https://www.historyproject.org/index.php/collections.

Boston Pride Collection
https://www.historyproject.org
"The Boston Pride Collection consists of papers (some originals and some photocopies), photographs, and ephemera from 1970 to 2008 related to the Boston Pride March and Rally, as well as materials from various celebrations and events during Pride week. The bulk of the collection is news coverage surrounding Pride Week preparations, goals, controversies, and summaries."

Homophile Union of Boston (HUB) Papers
https://www.historyproject.org
"The Homophile Union of Boston grew out of the Boston chapter of the Mattachine Society and was founded in late 1969 or early 1970. The organization's leadership was male, but there were also women members. The purpose of HUB was to provide a space for gay men and lesbians to talk about political and social issues affecting them and to offer a support network for members. The papers consist of organizational records, publications, and correspondence, and were compiled from material donated by officers of HUB, including Frank Morgan and Dick York."

Student Homophile League of Boston Collection
https://www.historyproject.org/
Active between 1969 and 1980, the Student Homophile League self-described as a "service group organizing social and political action for the college age community." First organized by MIT student Stan Tillotson in 1969, the organization became official in April of 1970 with Harry Phillips as the president. SHL was disbanded by the Vice President and the Secretary in December 1970, and then started with a new executive board and constitution in January 1971, as described in the letter of the new president William J. Canfield II. There was at times a great deal of dissent within the SHL, which can be seen in the disbanding and restarting of the organization in 1970, and scathing editorials and articles in Liberation, a SHL publication. The majority of the documents in the collection are either undated or are from 1970. The latest document is a letter from 1980 written to David Lynch and other members of the board requesting that all the membership lists

for the organization be destroyed and it appears that organization was defunct after that point.

Also notable in the collection is the great deal of overlap there was between various Boston homophile groups with the SHL being directly affiliated with Graduate Students Homophile Association of Harvard, B.U. Homophile Club, MIT Homophile Club, Gay Liberation Front, and also working with Eastern Regional Homophile Conference and the North American Conference of Homophile Organizations.

Boston Dyke March History and Archive Project

http://www.bostondykemarcharchives.org/

The Boston Dyke March History and Archive Project was founded by Jo Trigilio. The collection contains photographs, flyers, press articles, and event details from the first Boston Dyke March in 1995 to 2008. The Boston Dyke March is one of the oldest, most progressive, and one of the largest dyke marches in the U.S. The mission of the Boston Dyke March History and Archive Project is to collect and archive historically significant materials related to the Boston Dyke March. The purpose of the project is to make the history of the Boston Dyke March available to individuals, activists, educators, and researchers interested in LGBTQ+, feminist, gender, and/or social movement studies.

Digital Transgender Archive

360 Huntington Ave, Boston, MA 02115, https://www.digitaltransgenderarchive.net
Based at Northeastern University, the Digital Transgender Archive is a collaboration among dozens of colleges and universities that have collected and digitized materials related to transgender topics. Researchers can access oral interviews of transgender and gender non-conforming individuals. Its materials can be searched by topic, genre or collection. The Digital Transgender Archive holds items such as transgender newsletters and pamphlets, photographs, academic papers and publications, newspaper clippings and periodicals.

Collection descriptions drawn from "Collections," Digital Transgender Archive, accessed 2024, https://www.digitaltransgenderarchive.net/col.

Charlotte McLeod Collection

https://www.digitaltransgenderarchive.net/col/1831ck05t
"The items in the Charlotte McLeod Collection pertain to the transition and subsequent life of Charlotte McLeod, the second woman in the United States to undergo a gender realignment surgery that became known to the general public. The collection contains four photographs, one full autobiographical article, and thirty-seven news clippings. Nearly all of the materials discuss McLeod in relation to Christine Jorgensen, the first woman to become publicly known for receiving gender realignment surgery. Other topics include McLeod's employment history and paparazzi encounters."

Christine Jorgensen Collection

https://www.digitaltransgenderarchive.net/col/bc386j31v
"This collection features materials related to Christine Jorgensen, the first person in the United States to become publicly known for receiving gender realignment surgery. The collection includes newspaper clippings, one video, and photographs created between the 1950s and the early 1980s. Including both press coverage and candid photographs, the collection depicts Jorgensen's public life as well as her personal life."

East Coast FTM Group Organizational Records

https://www.digitaltransgenderarchive.net
"The East Coast FTM Group was a support group for FTMs––including transsexuals, crossdressers, and transgender people––and their partners that ran continuously from 1992 to 2015. The collection includes serial publications concerning the

group meetings, posters, press releases, and organization directories. The collection also contains correspondence between Ben Power and various other sources related to the East Coast FTM group. Also featured are photographs for Leslie Feinberg's book *Transgender Warriors*."

Metamorphosis
https://www.digitaltransgenderarchive.net/
"These newsletters and periodicals in the *Metamorphosis* collection were published by the Metamorphosis Medical Research Foundation and Rupert Raj from 198–1988. The Metamorphosis publications were intended to be a resource for female-to-male transsexuals. These objects discuss the issues of gender dysphoria, gender realignment surgery, and community acceptance. The newsletters and magazines provided the trans community with resources, personal stories, book and film reviews, and bulletins of important events and medical research pertaining to the trans community."

Phyllis Frye Collection
https://www.digitaltransgenderarchive.net/
"Phyllis Randolph Frye is the first openly transgender judge in the United States. She is also a U.S. Army veteran, a licensed engineer, an attorney, and a prominent trans activist. This collection includes 11 photographs and 1 certificate from the U.S. Army that document Frye's life journey between 1962 and 2006, reflecting her life before transitioning as well as her important role in the movement for transgender rights. This collection also features many documents including the International Bill of Gender Rights, an employer's handbook for addressing employees' gender transitioning, the Gay Agenda of the LGBTIQA Community of Houston, law reviews by Phyllis Frye, and biographical materials about Phyllis Frye."

TransSisters*: *The Journal of Transsexual Feminism
https://www.digitaltransgenderarchive.net/
"*TransSisters: The Journal of Transsexual Feminism* was created by Davina Anne Gabriel and published by Skyclad Publishing Co. throughout 1994 and 1995. Its statement of purpose reads: "In recognition of the fact that transsexual persons have been systematically silenced, marginalized, maligned and even brutalized, not only within mainstream society, but also even within feminist philosophy and culture, *TransSisters* " was created "to further the process of defining ourselves

and creating our own reality, rather than allowing others to do so." These periodicals feature articles, letters to the editor, book reviews, cartoons, photographs, and artwork. Issues covered include feminism, activism, the transgender movement, the women's movement, transphobia, discrimination, and civil rights."

Transvestia

https://www.digitaltransgenderarchive.net/

"*Transvestia* was an important periodical by and for transvestites published in the United States from 1960 to 1986. The magazine was founded by Virginia Prince who also served as editor-in-chief for the majority of its run until Carol Beecroft took over. *Transvestia* published life stories, articles, poetry, fiction, comics, photographs, and correspondence. This collection comprises 114 items including 111 unique issues and a small number of issue variations."

Northeastern University Archives and Special Collections-Boston's LGBTQA+ History

360 Huntington Ave, Boston, MA 02115, https://lgbtqahistory.library.northeastern.edu/

The Northeastern University Archives and Special collections "house numerous collections illustrating a diverse range of individuals, activism, and networks in the Boston LGBTQA community from the 1970s onwards." Some of the digitized and non-digitized materials include the AIDS Coalition to Unleash Power Boston chapter (ACT UP / Boston), the Boston Alliance of Gay and Lesbian Youth, Inc. (BAGLY), and the Massachusetts Gay and Lesbian Political Caucus records.

Collection descriptions drawn from "Collections – Boston's LGBTQA+ History," *Northeastern University Library* (blog), accessed 2024, https://lgbtqahistory.library.northeastern.edu/nucollections/.

G. Derrick Hodge papers

https://archivesspace.library.northeastern.edu/

"G. Derrick Hodge was a member of the AIDS Coalition to Unleash Power Boston (ACT UP/Boston) and Queer Nation/Boston in the early 1990's. Hodge served on ACT UP/Boston's discrimination, benefits, and finance working groups. ACT UP/Boston was founded in 1987 by activists Raymond Schmidt, Stephen Skuce, Donald Smith, and Paul Wychules to focus local efforts to speed up the development of AIDS treatments, educational programs, and prevention strategies. The membership was a diverse, nonpartisan group of people united in anger and committed to direct action to end the AIDS crisis. Queer Nation was an offshoot of ACT UP, created in response to elevated anti-gay and lesbian violence in the early 1990's."

ACT UP / Boston (Raymond Schmidt and Stephen Skuce) Collection
https://archivesspace.library.northeastern.edu/
"The AIDS Coalition to Unleash Power (ACT UP / Boston) was founded in 1987 by activists Raymond Schmidt, Stephen Skuce, Donald Smith, and Paul Wychules to focus local efforts to speed up the development of AIDS treatments, educational programs, and prevention strategies. The membership was a diverse, nonpartisan group of people united in anger and committed to direct action to end the AIDS crisis in Boston and throughout the country. The organization was most active from 1988 – 1994 during which time it held demonstrations, die-ins, sleep-ins, and vigils to increase public awareness of the AIDS epidemic."

Bisexual Resource Center Records
https://archivesspace.library.northeastern.edu/
"The Bisexual Resource Center is a Boston-based non-profit organization founded in 1985 as the East Coast Bisexual Network, Inc. [ECBN]. After attending the first conference on bisexuality in the northeast in 1984, Boston-area bisexual activists, including Robyn Ochs, Laura Sachs and Scott Lewis, organized a second regional conference the following year. With the profits from this conference, the East Coast Bisexual Network was founded as an umbrella group to facilitate organizing among bisexual groups on the East Coast. In the late 1980s, the East Coast Bisexual Network made HIV/AIDS education and activism a priority, as bisexual men and women were popularly accused of transferring the disease from gay males to lesbians and the straight population. In 1993, the organization expanded to include international bisexual organizations, and changed its name to the Bisexual Resource Center."

Bromfield Street Educational Foundation Records (featuring the *Gay Community News*)
https://archivesspace.library.northeastern.edu/
"The Bromfield Street Educational Foundation was originally established as the *Gay Community News* in 1973. Until the Bromfield Street Educational Foundation ceased operation in 1999 due to financial difficulties, the Gay Community News was one of the oldest, most progressive national newspapers in the gay commu-

nity. Eight Boston gays and lesbians started the newspaper in 1973 to create a community voice for gays and lesbians in the Boston area. In 1978, the Gay Community News became national in scope and distribution. The Bromfield Street Educational Foundation also sponsored other projects, including the Prisoners Project, an effort between 1975 and 1999 to support gays and lesbians in prison; OutWrite, an annual conference between 1990 and 1999 for gay and lesbian writers; *Off-the-Page*, a monthly reading series between 1993 and 1995 in Boston of gay and lesbian authors; and the Queer Progressive Organizing School, a forum in 1997 to organize progressive gay activists."

Boston Intercollegiate Lesbian and Gay Alliance Records
https://archivesspace.library.northeastern.edu/
"The Boston Intercollegiate Lesbian and Gay Alliance (BILGA) was created in 1983 as an umbrella organization for lesbian, gay, bisexual, and transgender student groups in the Boston area. The group coordinated student activism and community-building, provided support for fledgling student groups, and began an annual conference, the Northeast Lesbian and Gay Student Activist Conference. The conferences spawned the Northeast Lesbian and Gay Student Union, which began to run the event in 1985. The Boston Intercollegiate Lesbian and Gay Alliance disbanded in 1990."

William J. Canfield papers
https://archivesspace.library.northeastern.edu/
"William J. Canfield II was a gay activist in Boston and was involved in the Boston gay liberation movement between 1970 and 1975. In 197–1972, Canfield was president of Homophile Union of Boston (HUB). The Homophile Union of Boston was founded in 1969 by Frank Morgan in order to broaden awareness of gay lifestyles and seek civil rights for gays and lesbians. Along with John C. Graves, Canfield was a primary force behind the second attempt at collecting materials for a Boston Gay and Lesbian Archives. Additionally, he was a co-founder and business manager for the *Gay Community News* at its start."

Lesbian, Gay, Bisexual and Transgender Political Alliance of Massachusetts records
https://archivesspace.library.northeastern.edu/
"Founded as the Lesbian and Gay Political Alliance of Greater Boston (LGPAGB) in 1982, the Lesbian, Gay, Bisexual and Transgender Political Alliance of Massachu-

setts (LGBTPAM) is a political advocacy organization for gay and lesbian rights. The group has pursued causes relating to lesbian, gay, bisexual and transgender issues, such as funding for AIDS research and education, anti-discrimination legislation, legalization of same-sex unions, and the elimination of anti-gay violence. The founders of the organization hoped to increase the gay community's involvement in Boston's political process."

Gay and Lesbian Labor Activists Network records
https://archivesspace.library.northeastern.edu/
"The Gay and Lesbian Labor Activists Network is a Boston-based, non-profit, membership organization established in 1987. It campaigns for lesbian and gay liberation, fights against homophobia in the labor movement, and educates the lesbian and gay community about the importance of unions, organized labor, and the struggles of working people. The Gay and Lesbian Labor Activists Network has provided support to mainstream union campaigns, represented gay issues at various unions' meetings, and campaigned for domestic partner benefits and non-discrimination language in employers' policies. Among its greatest achievements is its role in forming a national organization for lesbian and gay labor rights, Pride At Work, in 1994. Pride At Work became a constituency group of The American Federation of Labor and Congress of Industrial Organizations (AFL-CIO) in 1997, and the Gay and Lesbian Labor Activists Network is now considered a local Pride At Work organization."

John C. Graves papers
https://archivesspace.library.northeastern.edu/
"John C. Graves was an activist involved in the gay liberation movement in Boston in the 1970s. Between 1964 and 1974, he was a philosophy professor at Massachusetts Institute of Technology. After coming out in 1972, he became actively involved in mental health, educational, and spiritual assistance programs for Boston's gay community. He was also active in student organizations and founded the Gay Academic Union of New England in 1974. In 1974, he left MIT and became a psychotherapist at the Homophile Community Health Service in Boston. An opera singer with the Boston Concert Opera, Graves was also a member of the Boston Gay Men's Chorus in the late 1980s. He was also involved with the formation of the Boston Center for Lesbians and Gay Men, serving as a steering and board member between 1987 and 1988."

Massachusetts Gay and Lesbian Political Caucus records

https://archivesspace.library.northeastern.edu/

"The Massachusetts Gay and Lesbian Political Caucus (the Caucus) was founded in 1973 to fight for social equality for the gay and lesbian community in Massachusetts. The Caucus was the first group within the gay and lesbian community to employ a lobbyist to work full-time on equal rights for gay men and lesbians. Initially, the Caucus focused on three statewide bills: to prohibit discrimination based on sexual preference in state employment, to prohibit discrimination statewide, and to amend the criminal code in regards to sexual conduct between consenting adults. The Caucus's focus has since grown to include issues such as same-sex marriage and parenthood. On November 15, 1989, the Caucus achieved a major victory when Governor Michael Dukakis signed the Gay and Lesbian Civil Rights Bill into law. The Caucus promotes participation from supporters of these issues by hosting annual lobbying events such as the Constituent Lobby Day, sending candidate and legislation endorsement letters, and collaborating with other local, state, and national gay and lesbian organizations."

Digital Commonwealth: Massachusetts Collections Online

https://www.digitalcommonwealth.org/

The Digital Commonwealth is useful for LGBTQ+ related research because it "provides access to photographs, manuscripts, books, audio recordings, and other materials of historical interest that have been digitized and made available by members of Digital Commonwealth, a statewide consortium of libraries, museums, archives, and historical societies from across Massachusetts."

Collection descriptions drawn from "Collections," Digital Commonwealth, accessed 2024, https://www.digitalcommonwealth.org/collections.

GenderServe

https://www.digitalcommonwealth.org/

"These publications of GenderServe, published by the Canadian "counseling, education, and research service" of the same name, are newsletters intended to provide information about and for the trans community. These newsletters include short bulletins on recent significant publications and upcoming events pertaining to the trans community, articles about the GenderServe, Gender Review, and FACT organizations and their reorganization."

GenderFlex: A Polygenderous Publication

https://www.digitalcommonwealth.org/

"This collection consists of items from the *GenderFlex: A Polygenderous Publication* collection hosted by Digital Transgender Archive. Information about the items has been provided by the holding institution so that they may be included in Digital Commonwealth."

Gender Review: The FACTual Newsletter

https://www.digitalcommonwealth.org/

"Starting with the first issue in June 1978, *Gender Review: The FACTual Newsletter* was the official publication for FACT, the Foundation for the Advancement of Canadian Transsexuals. Trans activist Rupert Raj started the Gender Review for trans men and women and also crossdressers. Articles covered a variety of topics and current events within the Canadian transsexual scene. The Gender Review sought equally to inform its readers of the community at large as well as offer resources for transsexual people in their everyday lives."

Grace and Lace Letter

https://www.digitalcommonwealth.org/

"*Grace and Lace Letter* was "an evangelical Christian publication for crossdressers, transgendered, and transsexuals" published in Jackson, Mississippi. This collection contains two quarterly international newsletters, a retrospective newsletter, and a brochure from the 1990s. These objects cover issues of religious acceptance and self-acceptance, and relate bible verses to personal experiences of crossdressing and trans-ing gender."

Mapping Boston's Former Gay Bars

https://storymaps.arcgis.com/

Created by Tessa Bahoosh, this project maps out all of Boston's former LGBTQ+ bars and clubs, from the 1920s to the 2020s. Bahoosh also surveyed LGBTQ+ individuals about their satisfaction and awareness of Boston's LGBTQ+ club scene.

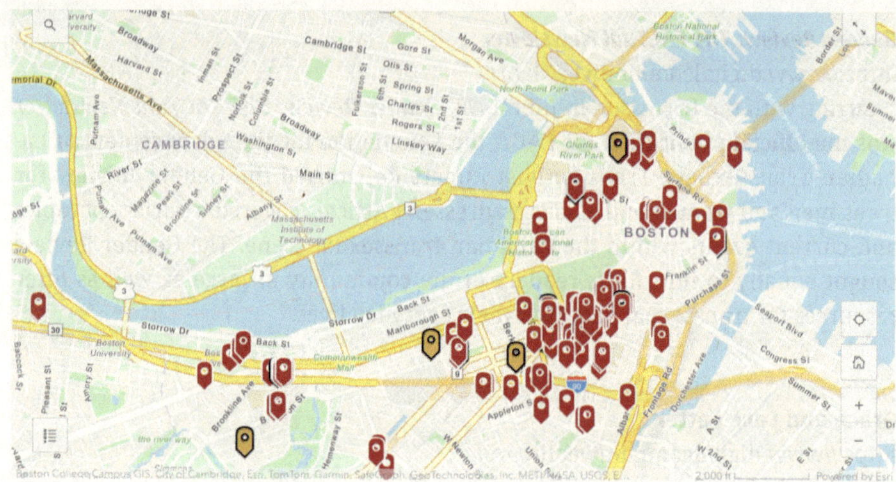

Source 58: Tessa Bahoosh, Screenshot of Map from Mapping Boston's Former Gay Bars, April 16, 2021, accessed May 1, 2024, ArcGIS Storymaps, https://arcg.is/yqXbj.

Collections in American Queer History

New York Public Library-Gay and Lesbian Collections & AIDS/HIV Collections

Stephen A. Schwarzman Building, Fifth Avenue at 42nd Street, New York, NY 10018–2788, https://www.nypl.org/lgbtqcollections.

"The Manuscripts and Archives Division of the New York Public Library holds over 100 collections pertaining to the history and culture of gay men and lesbians, and to the history of the AIDS/HIV epidemic." These papers and collections can only be accessed in person at the New York Public Library. The New York Public Library Digital Collections, however, also has wonderful resources on LGBTQ+ subjects.

Collection descriptions drawn from "Gay and Lesbian Collections & AIDS/HIV Collections," The New York Public Library, accessed 2024, https://drupal.nypl.org/about/divisions/manuscripts-division/lgbtq-collections.

Leo Adams papers, 1928–1952

https://archives.nypl.org/mss/16

"Leo Adams was a management executive with R.H. Macy & Co. in New York City from 1930 to 1965. Before Macy's he worked in the early motion picture theaters in Chicago and New York. Collection consists of Adams's correspondence, photographs and poetry. Correspondence is with friends and concerns the personal lives, cultural pursuits and careers of Adams and his circle during the Depression, World War II and post-war eras."

Arthur Bell papers, 1970–1978

https://archives.nypl.org/mss/250

"Arthur Bell was a journalist, writer for the *VILLAGE VOICE*, and gay rights activist. His papers include research notes, scripts and clippings of articles, minutes, memoranda and correspondence. The papers reflect his career as a free-lance journalist reporting on the gay liberation movement. Included is a script of an interview with Christopher Isherwood and papers relating to his activities as chairman of the publicity committee of the Gay Activists Alliance."

https://doi.org/10.1515/9783111560922-005

Copy Berg papers

https://archives.nypl.org/mss/3444

"Artist and gay rights activist Copy Berg was born Vernon E. Berg, III on July 10, 1951. He attended the United States Naval Academy from 1970–1974 and then served with the U.S. Navy Sixth Fleet in the Mediterranean. In 1975 the Navy sought to release him by General Discharge on grounds of homosexuality. Berg fought a highly publicized legal battle against the Navy but lost the case and was released in 1976. He settled in New York where he studied at Pratt Institute and launched his career as an artist. In 1986 Berg was diagnosed with human immunodeficiency virus (HIV), the cause of acquired immunodeficiency syndrome (AIDS). His subsequent artwork explored the social response to the AIDS epidemic, sexual politics and sadomasochism. Berg died of an AIDS-related illness on January 27, 1999. The Copy Berg Papers include correspondence of the artist, his friends and his family; records of Berg's service in the United States Navy and his discharge dispute; artwork; photographs; audio and video recordings; printed material and ephemera."

The GLBT Historical Society

989 Market St, San Francisco, CA 94103, https://www.glbthistory.org/
The GLBT Historical Society has a wide variety of digitized materials. Their collections span most of the mid to late 20th century and concern themes such as transgender politics, San Francisco LGBTQ+ activism, HIV/AIDS, oral histories, and queer and gender non-conforming social and recreational events.

Collection descriptions drawn from "Digital Collections," GLBT Historical Society, accessed 2024, https://www.glbthistory.org/digital-collections.

Dirk Alphin Collection of Valencia Rose videotapes
https://archive.org/
"Footage of performances at the Valencia Rose, an LGBTQ comedy club and performance space in San Francisco, circa 1985."

Bill Beardemphl papers
https://archive.org/
"Bill Beardemphl founded the Society for Individual Rights (SIR) in 1964; later, he would become a journalist, and in the 1980s was the owner of the *San Francisco Sentinel.*"

Larry Buttwinick papers
https://archive.org/
"Larry Buttwinick was a gay man who attended drag parties starting in the 1950s. This collection contains a film from one such party, circa 1965–1975."

Elsa Gidlow papers
https://archive.org/
"Elsa Gidlow (1898–1986) was a lesbian poet, philosopher, and woman of letters. Her book *On a Grey Thread* (1923) was the first collection of openly lesbian love poetry published in North America, and her autobiography, *Elsa: I Come With My Songs* (1986) was the first lesbian autobiography whose author did not publish under a pseudonym."

June Mazer Lesbian Archives

626 N. Robertson Blvd. West Hollywood, CA 90069
https://www.mazerlesbianarchives.org/digital-collections
The June Mazer Lesbian Archives is one of the largest lesbian archives in the United States. Its digital collection is limited, mostly focusing on lesbian feminist ephemera like clothing and buttons.

Collection descriptions drawn from "Digital Collections," June L. Mazer Lesbian Archives, accessed 2024, https://www.mazerlesbianarchives.org/digital-collections.

The Mazer T-Shirts

https://www.mazerlesbianarchives.org/t-shirt-collection
"The Mazer has hundreds of t-shirts from organizations, lesbian and feminist groups, activists, women and music festivals, and from some of the first women in men's fields."

The Mazer Buttons

https://www.mazerlesbianarchives.org/buttons-collection
"The Mazer has many buttons in the collection which include the Gay Games, marches, political, Wendy Averill, women (non-lesbian) and many other miscellaneous buttons."

Lesbian Herstory Archives

484 14th St, Brooklyn, NY 11215, https://lesbianherstoryarchives.org/
The Lesbian Herstory Archives has a wide collection of oral histories and interviews of lesbian activists and video recordings of lesbian events from the mid to late 20th century. Buttons, banners, photographs, and t-shirts are also available online to search.

Subject Files

https://lesbianherstoryarchives.org/collections/subject-files/
"[Herstory Archive's] 1,569 fascinating Subject Files fill the drawers of four five-drawer horizontal file cabinets plus overflow boxes. Think of these files as "Lesbians and . . . ". The first file is 'Abortion' and the last is 'Youth.' In between are

such topics as: “African-Ancestral Lesbians,” “Bars,” ‘Health Care,’ ‘Marriage,’ ‘Music Festivals,’ ‘Publishers,’ ‘Religion,’ ‘Theatre,’ and ‘Violence.’”

Spoken Word

https://lesbianherstoryarchives.org/collections/audio/

The archives include a physical collection of 3,000 oral herstory tapes, which collaborators have been working to digitize since 2012. Currently, the digital collection features audio of interviews, such as Joan Nelson interviewing Mable Hampton (1902–1989), who was an African American Lesbian activist. Additional material includes Audre Lorde’s public speeches, readings, and panel presentations. The collection continues to expand.

Periodicals, Newsletters & Zines

https://lesbianherstoryarchives.org/collections/periodicals/

“In addition to audio material, the archive hosts a broad and diverse selection of around 13,000 titles by or about Lesbians. The collection features US journals and glossy magazines from the 1940s, 50s and 60s; international journals, newspapers from the late 20th century, newsletters, and Zines. The staff is digitizing the material, making the material increasingly available for equitable research access.”

American Archive of Public Broadcasting

https://americanarchive.org/

The American Archive of Public Broadcasting is an online digital archive of the last 60 years of public broadcasting shows. This repository can be useful in locating interviews and radio and television programs concerning LGBTQ+ related themes. For example, by searching “LGBT” and limiting the date range, one can find a radio series produced in New York City in 1965 called, “The Homosexual: A New Minority.”

The ACT UP Oral History Project

https://actuporalhistory.org/

The ACT UP Oral History Project has hundreds of oral interviews with individuals involved in the ACT UP political organizations and/or who were directly affected by HIV/AIDS.

Women and AIDS

https://actuporalhistory.org/
This is a collection of oral interviews that concern women and the HIV/AIDS crisis.

Death and Dying

https://actuporalhistory.org/numerical-interviews/
This collection of oral interviews concern death and dying.

Affinity Groups

https://actuporalhistory.org/
This collection of oral interviews concern affinity groups and the AIDS/HIV crisis.

Independent Voices-LGBT collection

https://www.jstor.org/site/reveal-digital/independent-voices/lgbt/

According to the JSTOR website, the Independent Voices-LGBT collection "contains 25 publications that chronicle the birth of the Gay and Lesbian movements in the United States. The gay liberation movement of the 1970s saw political action explode through the National Gay and Lesbian Task Force, the Human Rights Campaign, the election of openly gay and lesbian representatives, and the first march on Washington for gay rights in 1979. Frustrated with the male leadership of most gay liberation groups and influenced by the feminist movement of the 1970s, lesbians formed their own collectives, music festivals, newspapers, bookstores, while calling for lesbian rights in mainstream feminist groups like the National Organization for Women (NOW)."

Outlook

https://www.jstor.org/site/reveal-digital/
"Published 1987 – 1992, *OUT/LOOK National Lesbian and Gay Quarterly* was racially inclusive, addressed gender complexity, focused on politics and culture alike, wrestled with topics that were controversial or not yet articulated, and emphasized visual work along with scholarly and creative writing. In a period before LGBT Studies and queer theory were established in the university, *OUT/LOOK* built a bridge between academic inquiry and broader community. *OUT/LOOK* led to the influential OutWrite conferences; the first of which was attended by over 1200 people."

Ozark Feminist Review

https://www.jstor.org/site/reveal-digital/

A feminist and queer publication dating back to 1991. The publication covers LGBTQ+ and women related topics nationally and throughout Missouri and Arkansas.

Philadelphia Gay News

https://www.jstor.org/site/reveal-digital/

"*Philadelphia Gay News* (PGN) is an LGBT newspaper in the Philadelphia area. The publication was founded in 1976 by Mark Segal, who was inspired by activist Frank Kameny when they met in 1970."

Storycorps Outloud

https://storycorps.org/

Storycorps is a non-profit organization that strives to record oral interviews of ordinary Americans. Its digital archive has hundreds of hours of interviews that concern LGBTQ+ topics. Researchers can narrow down their results with specific LGBTQ+ related search terms.

Library of Congress

https://www.loc.gov/

The Library of Congress has a vast array of digitized materials ranging from audio recordings, photographs, films, archived web pages, personal narratives and legislation. The Library of Congress also has a diverse collection of physical LGTBQ+ materials, but it is only accessible in person.

GenderWatch

https://about.proquest.com/en/products-services/genderwatch/

To access GenderWatch, subscription access needed.

"GenderWatch enhances gender and women's studies, and gay, lesbian, bisexual, and transgender (GLBT) research by providing authoritative perspectives from 1970 to present. This well-established and highly reviewed resource offers over 300 titles, with more than 250 in full-text, from an array of academic, radical, community and independent presses. Researchers and teachers may access more than 219,000 full articles on wide-ranging topics like sexuality, religion, societal roles, feminism, masculinity, eating disorders, healthcare, and the workplace.

"GenderWatch's strong collection of important, current titles provides users comprehensive support for gender, family, ethnic, and societal studies from both academic and grassroots perspectives. Users will find essential titles such as *Off Our Backs* (1970 to current) and *Transgender Tapestry*, international titles such as *Sister Namibia* and the *Australian Feminist Law Journal*, community newspapers such as Out & About and the *Windy City Times*, and many other diverse and interdisciplinary publications."

The Gay & Lesbian Review Worldwide

"*The Gay & Lesbian Review / Worldwide* (The G&LR) is a bimonthly magazine of history, culture, and politics targeting an educated readership of LGBT people, and their allies that publishes essays in a wide range of disciplines as well as reviews of books, movies, and plays."

The International Journal of Transgenderism

"*International Journal of Transgender Health*, together with its partner organization the World Professional Association for Transgender Health (WPATH), offers an international, multidisciplinary scholarly forum for publication in the field of transgender health in its broadest sense for academics, practitioners, policy makers, and the general population."

Center Happenings

"The Center fosters a welcoming environment where everyone is celebrated for who they are. We offer the LGBTQ communities of NYC advocacy, health and wellness programs; arts, entertainment and cultural events; recovery, parenthood and family support services."

Transgender Tapestry

"Founded by Merissa Sherrill Lynn, Transgender Tapestry was a magazine published from the late 1970s to the early 2000s first by the Tiffany Club and later by the International Foundation for Gender Education (IFGE). The publication went through several names changes including *The TV-TS Tapestry*, *Tapestry*, and *The Tapestry Journal*. This collection includes 106 issues including newsletters and quarterly periodicals from 1979 to 2008. Each issue of this magazine covers a variety of topics such as crossdressing, transsexualism, healthcare, political movements, film reviews, and more."

Archives of Sexuality and Gender: LGBTQ Culture and History Since 1940

https://www.gale.com/primary-sources/archives-of-sexuality-and-gender/collections/alliances
To access the Gale's Archives of Sexuality and Gender, subscription access needed.

"Including material from hundreds of major international activist organizations and local, grassroots groups, documents in this database present aspects of LGBTQ life in the second half of the twentieth century and beyond. Historical records of political and social organizations founded by LGBTQ individuals are included, as well as publications by and for lesbians and gays, and governmental responses to the AIDS crisis, personal correspondence and interviews with numerous LGBTQ individuals, and gay and lesbian newspapers from more than 35 countries, reports, policy statements, and more.

"With material dating back to the sixteenth century, researchers and scholars can examine how sexual norms have changed over time, health and hygiene, the development of sex education, the rise of sexology, changing gender roles, social movements and activism, erotica, and many other interesting topical areas. This growing archival program offers rich research opportunities across a wide span of human history."

The Mattachine Society of New York Records, 1951–1976

"This collection of records, spanning from 1951 to 1976, gives an overview of the American homophile movement (the gay rights movement including gay people and their allies) through the activities of the now-disbanded Mattachine Society of New York (MSNY). The Mattachine Society was one of the leaders of the gay rights movement in the latter half of the twentieth century, promoting its cause through education and other peaceful methods. It concentrated on assisting the gay community with mental health issues, educating the public about homosexuality, and lobbying to repeal discriminatory laws. The society came to be regarded as the authority on "the homosexual viewpoint" through its use of mass media."

Phyllis Lyon and Del Martin: Beyond the Daughters of Bilitis

"This collection covers the extensive work of Lyon and Martin in social movements for the advancement of the rights of women and sexual minorities – specifically, their work for, and leadership of, the LGBT movement and the modern women's rights movement both in San Francisco and across the United States. Their work illuminated issues such as police violence against gay youth, discrimination against LGBT persons in employment, enlightened responses to the victims of the AIDS crisis, and the backlash against affirmative action. A variety of materials in the collection, such as meeting minutes, notes, press clippings, reports, mailing lists, correspondence, and memoranda, showcase their work with the ACLU, the San Francisco Coalition for Human Rights, the Commission on Crime Control and Violence Protection, the Institute for the Advanced Study of Human Sexuality, the San Francisco Commission on the Status of Women, and the San Francisco Human Rights Commission."

National Transgender Library Collection

"The National Transgender Library and Archive was founded by Dallas Denny, an Atlanta–based activist, writer, and organizer in the transgender community. Denny was also the founder and served as executive director of the American Educational Gender Information Service (AEGIS), a non–profit advocacy group for individuals with gender dysphoria. AEGIS distributed materials and provided referrals to physicians, attorneys, clergy, and support groups within the community. In 1998, AEGIS was folded into Gender Education and Advocacy (GEA), a Georgia–based nonprofit."

Imperial Courts Collection

"The materials in the Imperial Courts Collection comprise one of sixteen collections of records from the ONE National Gay and Lesbian Archives, the world's largest repository of LGBTQ materials. These files document the lives of LGBTQ individuals from 1940 to 2012, the organizations they founded, the discrimination they faced, and the devastation of the AIDS crisis. Most of the items concern individuals or groups from California."

ACT UP: The AIDS Coalition to Unleash Power

"The AIDS Coalition to Unleash Power (ACT UP) was organized in 1987 to respond to the US government's handling of the AIDS crisis with aggressive, nonviolent direct action. Over the years, ACT UP agitated against sluggish government attention to the AIDS crisis, the high prices of AIDS medication, and the social stigma of AIDS.

"The materials in this collection span the period from 1980 to 2000, tracing the development of the AIDS crisis in the 1980s, the formation of ACT UP in 1987, and its grassroots activities through the 1990s. ACT UP by-laws and administrative manuals showcase the group's early history and structure, and financial records track operational expenses such as bills and postage, as well as fundraising auctions. Several years' worth of meeting minutes from the founding New York chapter of ACT UP are included in the collection, as well as minutes and materials from other US and international chapters. Correspondence found here reveals the nature of the group's dialogue and relationships with governments, corporations, other organizations, and the public."

Gay Activists Alliance, 1970–1983

"This collection of records gives an overview of the militant American homophile movement (the gay rights movement including gay people and their allies) from 1970 to 1983, particularly in New York, taken from the now-disbanded Gay Activists Alliance (GAA). The GAA was founded in response to the Stonewall riots of 1969, and it was intended to be a militant yet nonviolent organization advancing civil and social rights for gay people. It focused on attaining fair employment and housing, fought against laws specifically targeted at gays, and attempted to reduce police harassment. Members of the GAA also hoped to create a new gay culture, free from societal constraints." The collection itself is composed of four distinct categories: committee files, topical files, printed ephemera, and international lists of gay organizations and publications. The committee files are composed of records from various committees working within the Gay Activists Alliance."

Lesbian and Gay Christian Movement

"Originally founded in the United Kingdom in 1976 as the Gay Christian Movement, the Lesbian and Gay Christian Movement (LGCM) supported gay and lesbian Christians experiencing discrimination within their churches; urged denominations to reexamine doctrines concerning homosexuality; advocated for lesbian and gay civil rights both within the church and through legislation; and networked with other groups. In 2017, the LGCM merged with another group to become OneBodyOneFaith."

tion in the AIDS crisis, the importance of AIDS medication, and the [illegible] of AIDS.

The materials in this collection span the period from 1987 to 2000, covering the development of the AIDS crisis in the 1980s, the formation of ACT UP in 1987, and its progress activities through the 1990s. ACT UP by-laws and administrative materials show the group's early history and structure, and financial reports track operational expenses such as rent and postage as well as fundraising activities. Several years' worth of meeting minutes from the founding New York chapter of ACT UP are included in the collection, as well as materials and materials from other US and international chapters. Correspondence found here conveys the nature of the group's ideologies and relationships with gay advocates, coalitions, other organizations, and the public.

Gay Activists Alliance, 1970–1983

This collection of records offers an overview of the radical American homophile movement (the gay rights movement) including gay people and their allies from 1970 to 1983. Founded in New York City, activists who established Gay Activists Alliance (GAA). The GAA was founded in response to the Stonewall riots of 1969 and it was intended to be a militant yet nonviolent organization advocating civil and political rights for gay people. It focused on eliminating employment and housing discrimination, fought against laws and statutes that targeted gays, and attempted to reduce police harassment. Members of the GAA also helped to create a new gay culture free from societal prejudice. The collection itself is composed of four distinct categories: committee files, subject files, printed ephemera, and internal lists of gay organizations and publications. The committee files are comprised of records from various committees working within the Gay Activists Alliance.

Lesbian and Gay Christian Movement

Originally founded in the United Kingdom in 1976 as the Gay Christian Movement, the Lesbian and Gay Christian Movement (LGCM) supported gay and lesbian Christians experiencing discrimination within their churches, and it also campaigned to reexamine doctrines concerning homosexuality, advocating for lesbian and gay civil rights both within the church and through legislation. LGCM networked with other groups. In 2017, the LGCM merged with another group to become OneBodyOneFaith.[5]

Recommended Reading

Boag, Peter. *Same-Sex Affairs: Constructing and Controlling Homosexuality in the Pacific Northwest.* Berkeley: University of California Press, 2003.

Boyd, Nan. *Wide Open Town: A History of Queer San Francisco to 1965*. Berkeley: University of California Press, 2003.

Bronski, Michael. *A Queer History of the United States*. Boston: Beacon Press, 2011.

Capó, Julio. *Welcome to Fairyland: Queer Miami before 1940*. Chapel Hill: University of North Carolina Press, 2017

Cervini, Eric. *The Deviant's War: The Homosexual vs. the United States of America*. New York: Farrar, Straus and Giroux, 2020.

Chauncey, George. *Gay New York: Gender, Urban Culture, and the Making of the Gay Male World, 1890-1940*. New York: Basic Books, 2019.

Croix, St. Sukie. De la. *Chicago Whispers: A History of LGBT Chicago before Stonewall*. Madison: The University of Wisconsin Press, 2012.

Faderman, Lillian. *Odd Girls and Twilight Lovers: A History of Lesbian Life in Twentieth-Century America*. New York: Columbia University Press, 1991.

Frank, Miriam. *Out in the Union: A Labor History of Queer America*. Philadelphia: Temple University Press, 2014.

History Project. *Improper Bostonians: Lesbian and Gay History from the Puritans to Playland*. Boston: Beacon Press, 1998.

Johnson, David. *The Lavender Scare: The Cold War Persecution of Gays and Lesbians in the Federal Government*. Chicago: University of Chicago Press, 2004.

Kaiser, Charles. *The Gay Metropolis: The Landmark History of Gay Life in America*. New York: Grove Press, 2007.

Katz, Jonathan. *Gay American History: Lesbians and Gay Men in the U.S.A.* New York: Meridian, 1992.

Kennedy, Elizabeth Lapovsky, and Davis, Madeline D. *Boots of Leather, Slippers of Gold: The History of a Lesbian Community*. New York: Routledge, 1993.

Kirchick, James. *Secret City: The Hidden History of Gay Washington*. New York: Henry Holt, 2022.

Lopez, Russ. *The Hub of the Gay Universe: An LGBTQ History of Boston, Provincetown, and Beyond.* Boston: Shawmut Peninsula Press, 2018.

Manion, Jen. *Female Husbands: A Trans History*. Cambridge: Cambridge University Press, 2020.

Mesch, Rachel. *Before Trans: Three Gender Stories from Nineteenth-Century France*. Stanford: Stanford University Press, 2020.

Miller, Neil. *Out of the Past: Gay and Lesbian History from 1869 to the Present*. New York: Vintage Books, 1995.

Mumford, Kevin J. *Interzones: Black/White Sex Districts in Chicago and New York in the Early Twentieth Century*. New York: Columbia University Press, 1997.

Ryan, Hugh. *When Brooklyn Was Queer*. New York: St. Martin's Press, 2019.

Snorton, C. Riley. *Black on Both Sides: A Racial History of Trans Identity*. Minneapolis: University of Minnesota Press, 2017.

Stryker, Susan. *Transgender History: The Roots of Today's Revolution*. New York: Seal Press, 2017.

https://doi.org/10.1515/9783111560922-006

Appendix: Timeline of American LGBTQA+ Rights and Events

1917	The Immigration Act of 1917 is passed. Homosexual immigrants are banned from entering into the United States.
1924	Henry Gerber establishes the Society for Human Rights, the nation's first gay rights organization. The organization dissolved after two years.
1948	Alfred Kinsey's *Sexual Behavior in the Human Male* is published. Its survey data suggests that approximately 10% of American males are homosexual and that a third of all men have had at least one same-sex sexual experience with another man.
1950	Harry Hay forms the Mattachine Society.
1952	The American Psychiatric Association's diagnostic manual designates homosexuality as a personality disorder.
1952	Christine Jorgensen, a former World War Two veteran, travels to Denmark to undergo sex reassignment surgery. She would become an instant celebrity upon her return to America. Jorgensen is widely viewed as one of the first well-known American transgender women in the country.
1953	President Dwight D. Eisenhower issues Executive Order 10450 which fired suspected lesbian and gay men and women from federal employment and denied queer applicants federal jobs.
1955	Daughters of Bilitis, the first lesbian rights organization, is founded in San Francisco.
1958	The Supreme Court ruled in One, Inc. v. Olesen that the publishing, distributing and writing of homosexuality is protected under the first amendment.
1961	Illinois becomes the first state to decriminalize homosexuality.
1965	On July 4th, dozens of LGBTQ+ activists gather in front of Independence Hall in Philadelphia and demand equal rights for queer Americans.
1966	The Compton's Cafeteria riot occurs when drag queens and transgender women riot in response to police harassment. This marks the beginning of transgender activism in San Francisco.
1969	Police raid the Stonewall Inn, a gay bar in Greenwich Village, New York City. In the immediate aftermath of the raid, bar patrons violently retaliated against the police, sparking the modern gay rights movement in America.
1970	LGBTQ+ activists organize the first gay pride parade in New York City to commemorate the Stonewall riots.
1970	Maryland becomes the first state to ban same-sex marriage.
1973	The American Psychiatric Association removes homosexuality from its list of mental disorders.
1979	Over a hundred thousand LGBTQ+ individuals stage the first National March on Washington for Lesbian and Gay Rights.
1980	The HIV/AIDS epidemic begins in the United States predominantly affecting hundreds of thousands of gay men and transgender women.
1982	Wisconsin becomes the first state to ban discrimination based on sexual orientation.

https://doi.org/10.1515/9783111560922-007

1993 President Bill Clinton enacts the "Don't Ask, Don't Tell" policy banning openly gay and lesbian Americans from serving in the military.

1996 President Bill Clinton signs the Defense of Marriage Act, defining marriage as a legal union between a man and a woman while banning same-sex marriage.

2004 Massachusetts becomes the first U.S. state to legalize same-sex marriage.

2012 Tammy Baldwin of Wisconsin becomes the first openly gay woman elected to the Senate.

2015 In a 5-4 decision, the U.S. Supreme Court legalizes same-sex marriage throughout the United States.

2020 In a 6-3 decision, the U.S. Supreme Court rules that Title VII of the Civil Rights Act of 1964 protects gay and transgender employees against discrimination.

2022 The Respect for Marriage Act is signed into law by President Joe Biden, overturning the Defense of Marriage Act and requires the federal government and all U.S. states to recognize same-sex and interracial marriages.

Index

https://doi.org/10.1515/9783111560922-008

Editor's Statement

As of 2024, **Sam Hurwitz** was a PhD student in the Boston College History Department. Sam's research interests concern Boston history, LGBTQ+ history and 20th-century American history. Previously, they graduated from the University of Wisconsin at Madison in 2017 with a degree in History.

https://doi.org/10.1515/9783111560922-009